This Christmas Coloring Book
Belongs To:

____

____

Write and Draw to Express Yourself

Date: _______ / ____ / ____

Write and Draw to Express Yourself

Date: ___/___/___

Date: _____ / ___ / _____

Write and Draw to Express Yourself

Date:

Write and Draw to Express Yourself

Date: ____ / ___ / ___

Write and Draw to Express Yourself

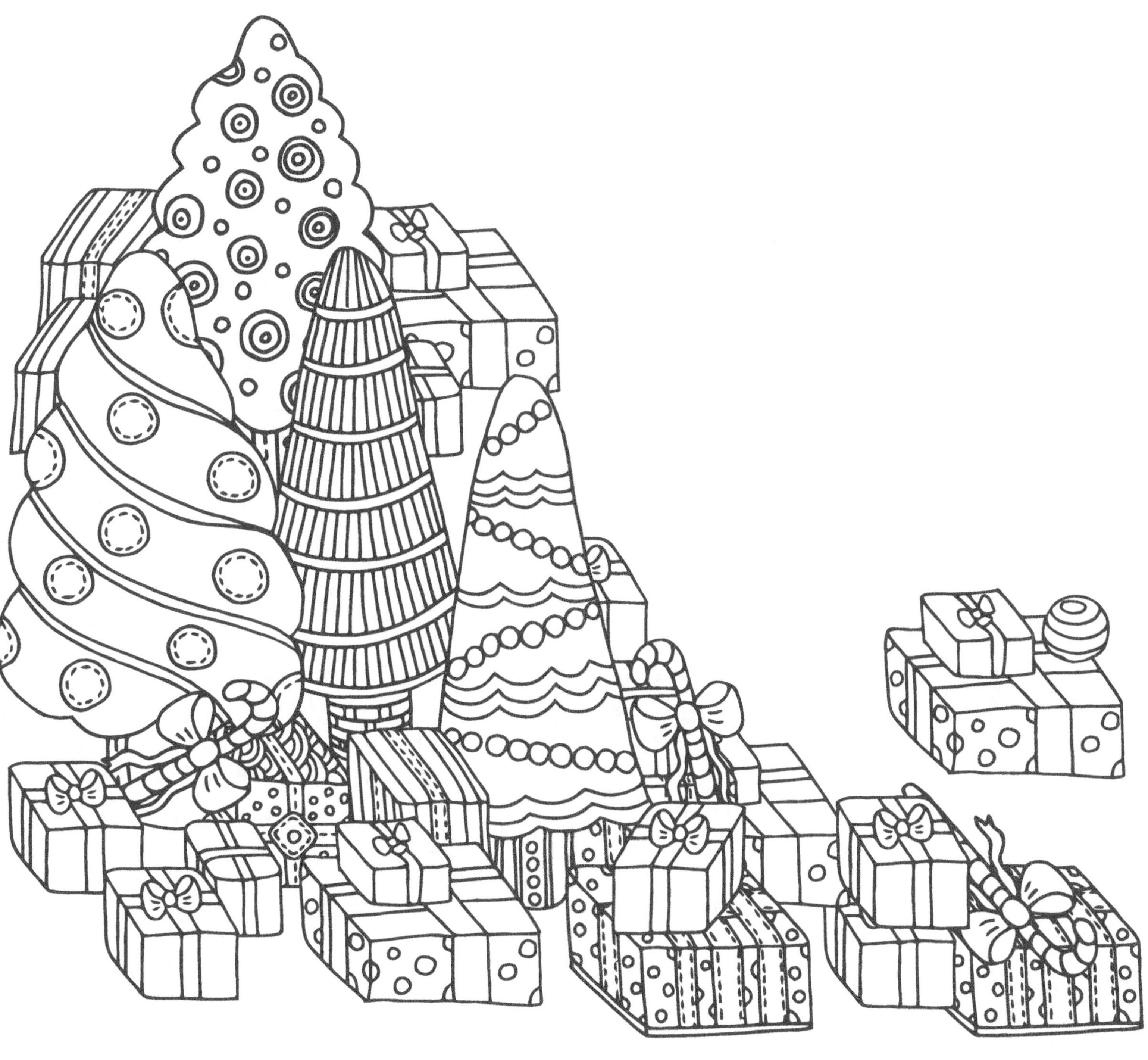

Write and Draw to Express Yourself

Date: _____ / ___ / ___

Write and Draw to Express Yourself

Date: /   /

Date: ______/______/______

Write and Draw to Express Yourself

Date:
Xmas

Write and Draw to Express Yourself

Date:

Write and Draw to Express Yourself

Date: ___ / ___ / ___

Write and Draw to Express Yourself

Date: ___ / ___ / ___

Christmas
Time

Write and Draw to Express Yourself

Date: _______ / ____ / ____

Date: ___/___/___

Write and Draw to Express Yourself

Write and Draw to Express Yourself

Date: ___ / ___ / ___

Date: _______ / ___ / _______

Merry Christmas

Write and Draw to Express Yourself

Date: ___ / ___ / ___

Date: _____ / ___ / _____

Write and Draw to Express Yourself

Date: ___ / ___ / ___

Write and Draw to Express Yourself

Date: ___ / ___ / ___

Write and Draw to Express Yourself

Date: ___ / ___ / ___

Write and Draw to Express Yourself

Date: ___/___/___

Write and Draw to Express Yourself

Date: ___ / ___ / ___

Date: ___/___/___

Write and Draw to Express Yourself

Date: _______ / ___ / ______

Write and Draw to Express Yourself

Date: ___/___/___

Write and Draw to Express Yourself

The
Magic of
Christmas

Write and Draw to Express Yourself

Write and Draw to Express Yourself

Date: ___/___/___

Write and Draw to Express Yourself

Date: _______ / _______ / _______

Write and Draw to Express Yourself

Date: _______ / ___ / _______

Write and Draw to Express Yourself

Date: ___ / ___ / ___

Write and Draw to Express Yourself

Date: ___ / ___ / ___

Write and Draw to Express Yourself

Date:

Write and Draw to Express Yourself

Write and Draw to Express Yourself

Date: ___ / ___ / ___

Write and Draw to Express Yourself

peace
&
joy

Date: ___/___/___

Write and Draw to Express Yourself

Date: ___ / ___ / ___

Write and Draw to Express Yourself

Write and Draw to Express Yourself

Date: ___/___/___

Date: ___/___/___

Write and Draw to Express Yourself

Write and Draw to Express Yourself

Date: ___ / ___ / ___

Date: _____/____/_____

Write and Draw to Express Yourself

Date: _____ / ___ / ___

Write and Draw to Express Yourself

Date: _____ / _____ / _____

Write and Draw to Express Yourself

Date: _____ / ___ / ___